2x10

Usborne
Times Tables
Activity Book

Rosie Hore

3x5

Illustrated by
Luana Rinaldo

Designed by
Holly Lamont

2x3

Education consultant: Sheila Ebbutt

You can check the answers to the puzzles at the back of the book.

What are times tables?

Times tables are lists of multiplication questions and answers. Once you know them, you can multiply the numbers from 1 to 12 much more quickly and easily.

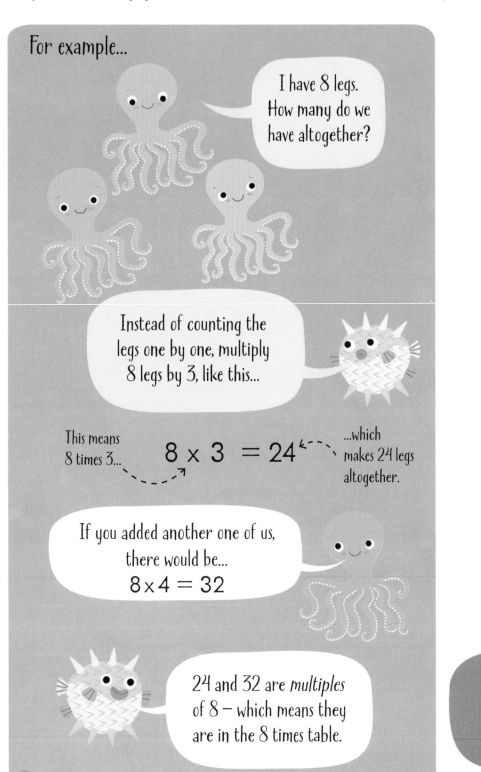

For example...

I have 8 legs. How many do we have altogether?

Instead of counting the legs one by one, multiply 8 legs by 3, like this...

This means 8 times 3...

$8 \times 3 = 24$

...which makes 24 legs altogether.

If you added another one of us, there would be...
$8 \times 4 = 32$

24 and 32 are *multiples* of 8 – which means they are in the 8 times table.

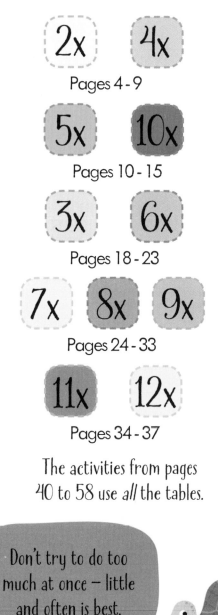

You'll find the tables on the pages listed below, but you can work through them in any order you like.

2x   4x

Pages 4 - 9

5x   10x

Pages 10 - 15

3x   6x

Pages 18 - 23

7x   8x   9x

Pages 24 - 33

11x   12x

Pages 34 - 37

The activities from pages 40 to 58 use *all* the tables.

Don't try to do too much at once – little and often is best.

Tips and tricks

This book is full of activities to help you learn the tables from 2x to 12x. There are lots of tips and tricks along the way.

Try saying the tables out loud before you start each page. It might help you remember them.

7, 14, 21...

4, 8, 12, 16...

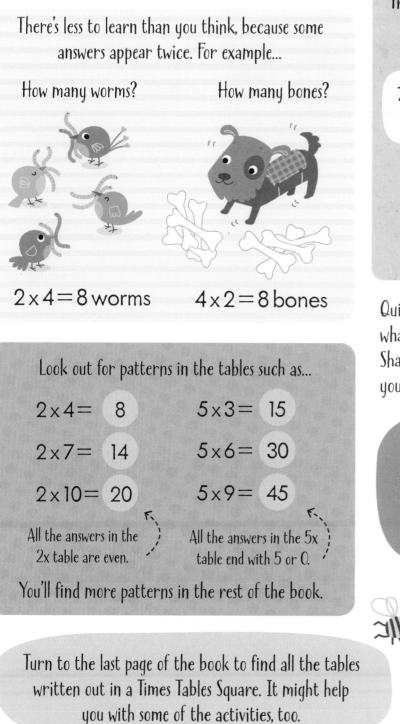

There's less to learn than you think, because some answers appear twice. For example...

How many worms?

How many bones?

$2 \times 4 = 8$ worms

$4 \times 2 = 8$ bones

Look out for patterns in the tables such as...

$2 \times 4 =$ 8 $5 \times 3 =$ 15

$2 \times 7 =$ 14 $5 \times 6 =$ 30

$2 \times 10 =$ 20 $5 \times 9 =$ 45

All the answers in the 2x table are even.

All the answers in the 5x table end with 5 or 0.

You'll find more patterns in the rest of the book.

Quick Quizzes let you check what you've learned so far. Shade in the star for each quiz you complete.

Don't worry if you get stuck. Just take a look at the answer pages at the back of this book...

...or flip back to the page with the table written out.

Turn to the last page of the book to find all the tables written out in a Times Tables Square. It might help you with some of the activities, too.

2x

2x1 = 2

2x2 = 4

2x3 = 6

2x4 = 8

2x5 = 10

2x6 = 12

2x7 = 14

2x8 = 16

2x9 = 18

2x10 = 20

2x11 = 22

2x12 = 24

The 2x table can help you count in pairs.

Fill in the missing numbers.

How many worms?

2 x 4 = ☐

How many acorns?

2 x 6 = ☐

How many wings?

2 x ☐ = ☐

Join up the questions and answers to match each bird to its nest.

24   18   14

2 x 9   2 x 7   2 x 12

You can check the complete table on the left if you get stuck.

These butterflies fly in pairs. Draw in the butterfly nets to catch...

8 butterflies

16 butterflies

10 butterflies

This frog will only eat flies with numbers in the 2x table. Draw an X over each fly that gets eaten.

Even numbers taste best.

6 8 1 10
3   4
7   9
12   6
2 5 11

Tip: Multiplying by 2 is the same as doubling.

This spider can spin 2 webs every hour. How many can it spin in 8 hours? Circle the correct answer.

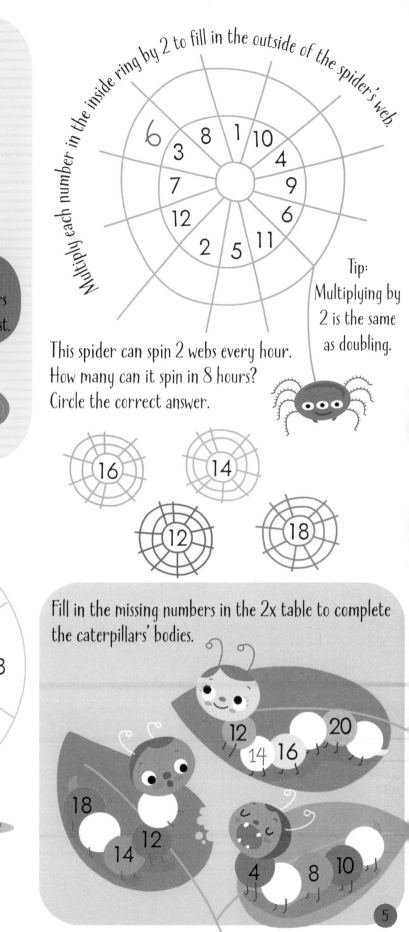

16   14

12   18

Solve the puzzles below and shade in the answers on the snail's shell, following the key.

22
20 6 14
8 14 10
2 18
10 12 2 24 18
24 16
20 6 4 2
22
14 8 20

2x1, 2x2, 2x3, 2x4 = blue
2x5, 2x6, 2x7, 2x8 = green
2x9, 2x10, 2x11, 2x12 = yellow

Fill in the missing numbers in the 2x table to complete the caterpillars' bodies.

12   20
14 16

18
12
14

4 8 10

5

4x

4 x 1 = 4

4 x 2 = 8

4 x 3 = 12

4 x 4 = 16

4 x 5 = 20

4 x 6 = 24

4 x 7 = 28

4 x 8 = 32

4 x 9 = 36

4 x 10 = 40

4 x 11 = 44

4 x 12 = 48

To multiply a number by 4, try doubling it twice.

Fill in the missing numbers.

How many legs?

4 x 3 = ☐

How many bones?

4 x ☐ = 8

How many spots?

4 x ☐ = ☐

Black out the two incorrect answers on each paw print, leaving the correct answer behind.

50 14 40
4 x 10

24 18 32
4 x 6

20 24 30
4 x 5

42 32 30
4 x 8

Solve the puzzles on each stand at the pet show and write the number on the prize-winning iguanas' medals.

4 x 9

4 x 7

4 x 12

4 x 11

Find a route for the tortoise to eat through every multiple of 4. He can go up, down, left or right, but doesn't like the taste of anything not in the 4x table.

Solve these questions, then shade in the answers on the parrot's feathers following the code below.

4 × 3	4 × 4	4 × 1	4 × 2
4 × 7	4 × 5	4 × 6	4 × 9
4 × 11	4 × 12	4 × 8	4 × 10

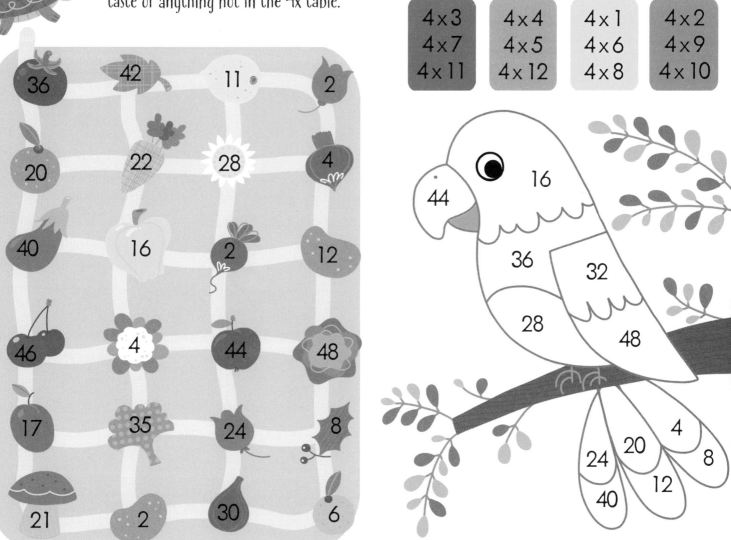

The number on each ball equals the two numbers below it multiplied together.
Can you fill in the missing numbers?

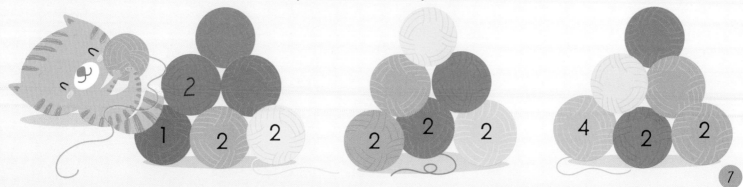

2x 4x

Which shirt matches all the clues?

The player's
number is:
Smaller than 4 x 8
Bigger than 2 x 4
Not equal to 4 x 7

6   28   10   34

Find the answers on the line that match the questions below. Which piece of clothing is left?

2 x 3   4 x 9   4 x 12
2 x 7   4 x 10   4 x 11
2 x 11   2 x 9   4 x 5

6   36   20   14

Finish the laundry list.
How many pairs...?

20 sports socks = ☐ pairs

10 gloves = ☐ pairs

8 mittens = ☐ pairs

16 hiking socks = ☐ pairs

Each box of laundry soap lasts for 2 weeks. Each bottle of fabric softener lasts for 4 weeks. How many bottles and boxes would you use in...

12 weeks = ☐ boxes and ☐ bottles

16 weeks = ☐ boxes and ☐ bottles

24 weeks = ☐ boxes and ☐ bottles

Can you find the sock that's been hung on the wrong peg?

Socks with spots should go on numbers which are in the 2 times table *and* the 4 times table.

Socks with stripes should go on numbers which are in the 2 times table only.

Join up the shoes with the boxes they go into.

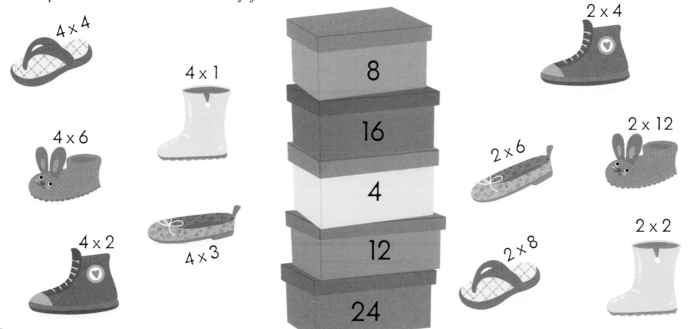

4 x 4

4 x 1

4 x 6

4 x 2

4 x 3

8

16

4

12

24

2 x 4

2 x 12

2 x 6

2 x 2

2 x 8

5x

5 x 1 = 5
5 x 2 = 10
5 x 3 = 15
5 x 4 = 20
5 x 5 = 25
5 x 6 = 30
5 x 7 = 35
5 x 8 = 40
5 x 9 = 45
5 x 10 = 50
5 x 11 = 55
5 x 12 = 60

Numbers in the 5 times table end in 5 or 0.

Fill in the missing numbers.

How many lights?

$5 \times 3 = \boxed{}$

How many dials?

$5 \times 4 = \boxed{}$

How many wheels?

$5 \times \boxed{} = \boxed{}$

When you give these robots a number, they multiply it by 5.
Fill in the missing numbers and answers.

$\boxed{5} \times 5 = \boxed{25}$

$\boxed{} \times 5 = \boxed{55}$

$\boxed{10} \times 5 = \boxed{}$

$\boxed{} \times 5 = \boxed{45}$

$\boxed{} \times 5 = \boxed{35}$

Battery

Starting at the battery, join together all the multiples of 5. Which robot does the trail lead to? Find it and shade it in.

40 25 5 45 48

51 39 14 20 62

7 29 6 10 9

82 52 60 55 11

12 35 50 47 44

30 15 33 23 17

10x

10 x 1 = 10
10 x 2 = 20
10 x 3 = 30
10 x 4 = 40
10 x 5 = 50
10 x 6 = 60
10 x 7 = 70
10 x 8 = 80
10 x 9 = 90
10 x 10 = 100
10 x 11 = 110
10 x 12 = 120

To multiply any number by 10, just add a 0.

Fill in the missing numbers.

How many spikes?

10 x 5 = ☐

How many teeth?

10 x 6 = ☐

How many eyes?

10 x ☐ = ☐

There are 10 mini-monsters in each puddle of slime. How many are there in...

7 puddles? ....

9 puddles? ....

12 puddles? ....

Each squirt of anti-monster mist scares away 10 monsters. How many squirts would you need to scare...

110 monsters? ....

50 monsters? ....

20 monsters? ....

A big monster can gobble 10 mini-monsters in a minute. How many can it gobble in...

3 minutes? ....

6 minutes? ....

10 minutes? ....

These mini-monsters pass messages by touching feelers. Can you pass a message from one red monster to the other, by shading in all the multiples of 10?

115
42
103
30
40
15
50
12
100
20
120
100
55
23
110
70
18
115
70
60
75
29
110
35
82
97
80
105
35
15
40
77
50
22
65
36
80
25
33
90
102
22
57
120

Swat all the monsters in the 10 times table by drawing an X over them. Be as quick as you can!

100
5
110
120
38
40
50
58
10
90
103
60
18
115
20
70
30

5x   10x

Circle the question on each rocket that matches the answer on the flame beneath.

5 x 10
5 x 11
5 x 12

60

5 x 7
5 x 8
5 x 9

45

10 x 8
10 x 9
10 x 10

90

10 x 3
10 x 4
10 x 5

30

It takes five days to fly between each planet. Can you figure out these puzzles?

How long will it take to reach Planet Zatt from Planet Zip?

5 x 4 = ☐ days

How long is the flight from Planet Zatt to Planet Zitch?

5 x ☐ = ☐ days

Planet Zip

Planet Zong

Planet Zam

Planet Zewt

Planet Zatt

Which alien has been chosen for the space mission? The alien's number is...

In the 5 times table
Bigger than 10 x 3
Smaller than 5 x 8

Circle the correct alien.

32

18

35

40

30

15

Fill in the missing numbers in the craters.

$5 \times = 15$

$10 \times = 60$

$ \times 9 = 90$

$5 \times 7 = $

How many planets could I travel between in 25 days?

How long does it take to fly from Planet Zop to Planet Zong? days

How long will it take to deliver a letter from Planet Zing to Planet Zip? days

Planet Zitch

Planet Zeep

Planet Zop

Planet Zwug

Planet Zing

2 x 2 =

2 x 4 =

2 x 6 =

2 x 11 =

2 x 3 =

2 x 1 =

2 x 10 =

2 x 12 =

2 x 9 =

2 x 5 =

2 x 8 =

2 x 7 =

Score

Star

12

4 x 10 =

4 x 7 =

4 x 5 =

4 x 2 =

4 x 6 =

4 x 12 =

4 x 9 =

4 x 11 =

4 x 3 =

4 x 1 =

4 x 4 =

4 x 8 =

Score

Star

12

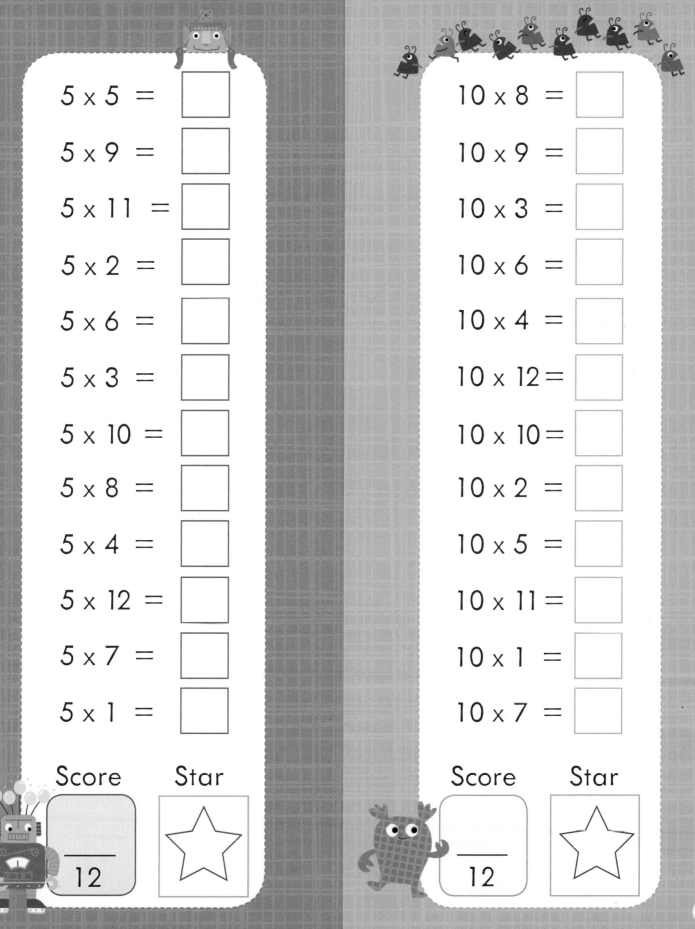

5 x 5 =

5 x 9 =

5 x 11 =

5 x 2 =

5 x 6 =

5 x 3 =

5 x 10 =

5 x 8 =

5 x 4 =

5 x 12 =

5 x 7 =

5 x 1 =

Score

$\dfrac{}{12}$

Star

10 x 8 =

10 x 9 =

10 x 3 =

10 x 6 =

10 x 4 =

10 x 12 =

10 x 10 =

10 x 2 =

10 x 5 =

10 x 11 =

10 x 1 =

10 x 7 =

Score

$\dfrac{}{12}$

Star

3x

3 x 1 = 3

3 x 2 = 6

3 x 3 = 9

3 x 4 = 12

3 x 5 = 15

3 x 6 = 18

3 x 7 = 21

3 x 8 = 24

3 x 9 = 27

3 x 10 = 30

3 x 11 = 33

3 x 12 = 36

You can use the 3x table to count quickly in threes.

Fill in the missing numbers.

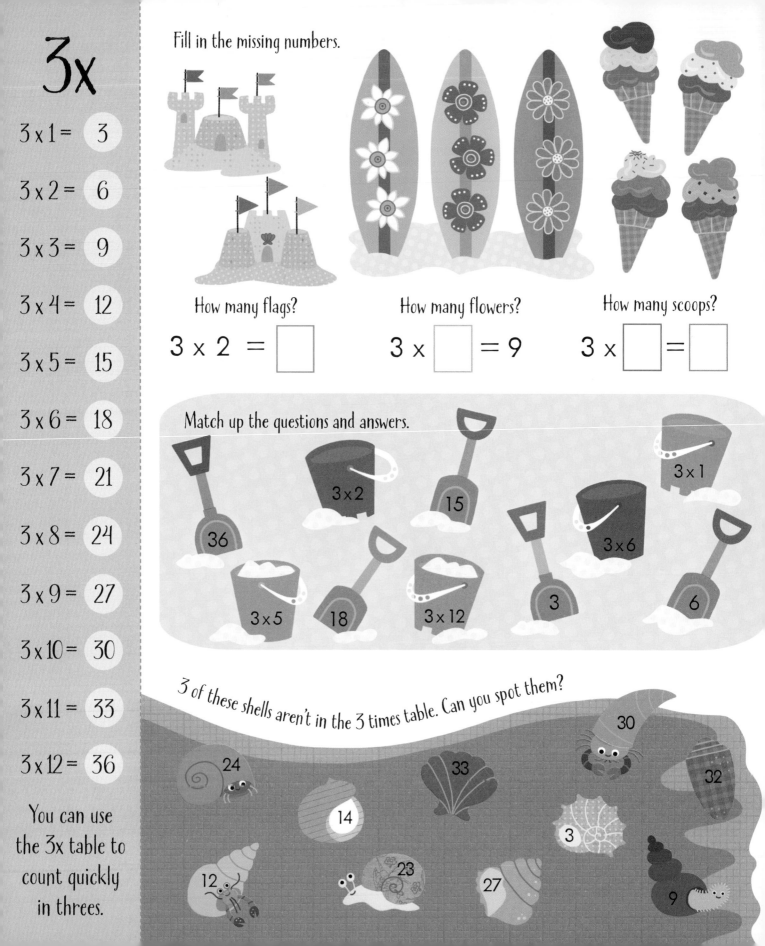

How many flags?

3 x 2 = ☐

How many flowers?

3 x ☐ = 9

How many scoops?

3 x ☐ = ☐

Match up the questions and answers.

3 x 2   15   3 x 1

36   3 x 6

3 x 5   18   3 x 12   3   6

3 of these shells aren't in the 3 times table. Can you spot them?

24   33   30   32

14   3

12   23   27   9

Shade the stripes on the deckchairs to match the puzzles on the beach balls.

15 24 21

6 3 9

3 x 7
3 x 5
3 x 9

3 x 4
3 x 10
3 x 2

3 x 3
3 x 1
3 x 11

30 36 33

18 27 12

3 x 12 3 x 6
3 x 8

Finish the number pattern on the footprints in the sand.

12

36

21 24

6

3

6x

6 x 1 = 6

6 x 2 = 12

6 x 3 = 18

6 x 4 = 24

6 x 5 = 30

6 x 6 = 36

6 x 7 = 42

6 x 8 = 48

6 x 9 = 54

6 x 10 = 60

6 x 11 = 66

6 x 12 = 72

Numbers in the 6 times table are always even.

Fill in the missing numbers.

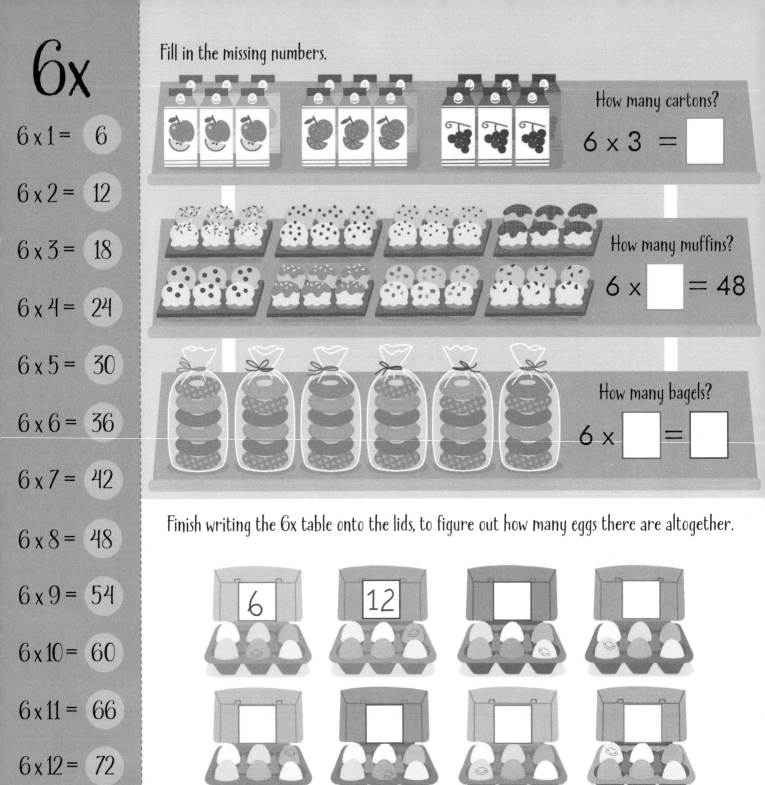

How many cartons?

6 x 3 = ☐

How many muffins?

6 x ☐ = 48

How many bagels?

6 x ☐ = ☐

Finish writing the 6x table onto the lids, to figure out how many eggs there are altogether.

Finish the shopping list for 6 people.

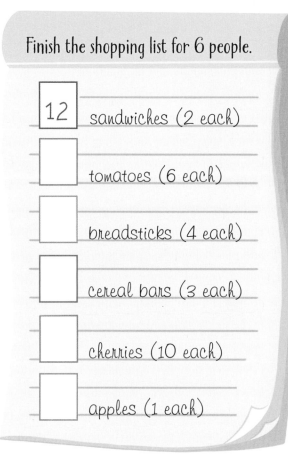

12	sandwiches (2 each)
	tomatoes (6 each)
	breadsticks (4 each)
	cereal bars (3 each)
	cherries (10 each)
	apples (1 each)

Each kind of cookie is shared equally between 6 plates. Draw the cookies there would be on 1 plate.

18 coconut cookies

12 chocolate cookies

24 cherry cookies

Fill the basket by drawing in all the groceries that are in the 6x table.

3x 6x

Circle the shuttlecocks which are in both the 3x table *and* the 6x table.

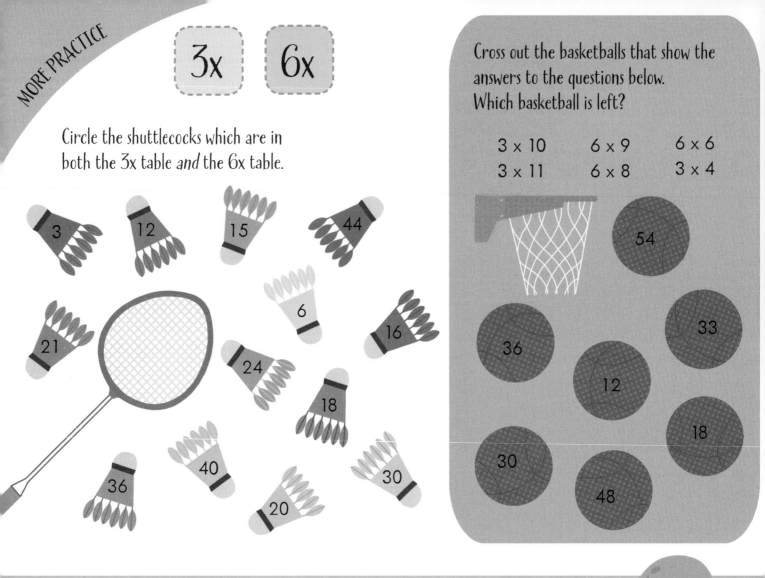

Cross out the basketballs that show the answers to the questions below. Which basketball is left?

3 × 10	6 × 9	6 × 6
3 × 11	6 × 8	3 × 4

Circle the answers to the questions, then join the circles you've made from smallest to biggest to find the kayak's route around the obstacles.

6 × 5
3 × 7
3 × 8
6 × 3
3 × 11
6 × 12
6 × 2
6 × 7
3 × 3

START

17
46
24
22
9
34
12
21
18
40

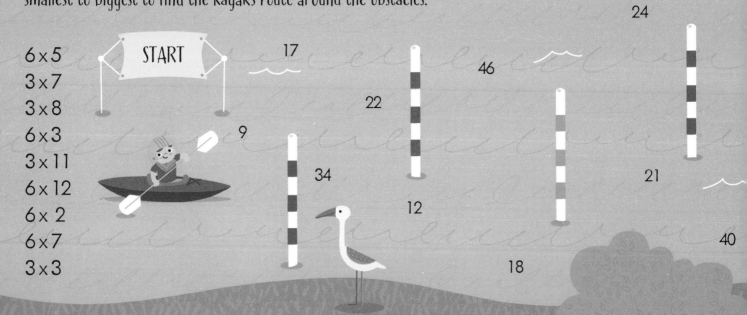

The number on each ball equals the two numbers below it multiplied together. Can you fill in the missing numbers?

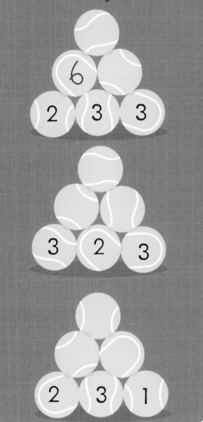

When the skiers pass a flag, they win the number of points on that flag. How many points has each skier won?

Start!

3
6
6
6
3
3
3
3
6
6
3
6
6
3
3

POINTS

POINTS

25
30
FINISH
103
72
52
75
42
33
32

23

7x

7 x 1 = 7

7 x 2 = 14

7 x 3 = 21

7 x 4 = 28

7 x 5 = 35

7 x 6 = 42

7 x 7 = 49

7 x 8 = 56

7 x 9 = 63

7 x 10 = 70

7 x 11 = 77

7 x 12 = 84

To remember
7 x 8, say
5, 6, 7, 8:
56 = 7 x 8.

Fill in the missing numbers.

How many bells?

7 x 2 = ☐

How many fish?

7 x ☐ = ☐

It takes the Arctic explorers 7 days to trek between each checkpoint on their route.

How long will it take from base camp to get to...

Checkpoint 3?

☐ days

Checkpoint 5?

☐ days

Checkpoint 7?

☐ days

Base camp

POLE

Where will they be after...

63 days?

Checkpoint ☐

77 days?

Checkpoint ☐

Fill in the missing numbers to complete the igloo.

7 x 8 =

7 x 2 =

7 x 10 =

7 x 9 =

7 x 12 =

7 x 7 =

7 x 4 =

7 x 6 =

This fisherwoman only catches fish in the 7 times table. Circle each fish she'll catch below.

Connect the dots in the 7 times table, from smallest to biggest, to see who's swimming under the ice.

7

84

14

77

21

35   28

42

49

56

63

70

67

56

21

20

42

44

63

35

52

84

70

8x

8 x 1 = 8
8 x 2 = 16
8 x 3 = 24
8 x 4 = 32
8 x 5 = 40
8 x 6 = 48
8 x 7 = 56
8 x 8 = 64
8 x 9 = 72
8 x 10 = 80
8 x 11 = 88
8 x 12 = 96

Look at the last digit of each answer. Can you spot a pattern?

Fill in the missing numbers.

How many tentacles?

8 x 3 = [ ]

How many spikes?

8 x [ ] = [ ]

Finish filling in the coral reef, so questions and answers are the same shades.

96

64

40

80

8 x 10

64

72

40

8 x 5

88

8 x 2

64

Circle the seahorse with the smallest number, and the clownfish with the biggest number.

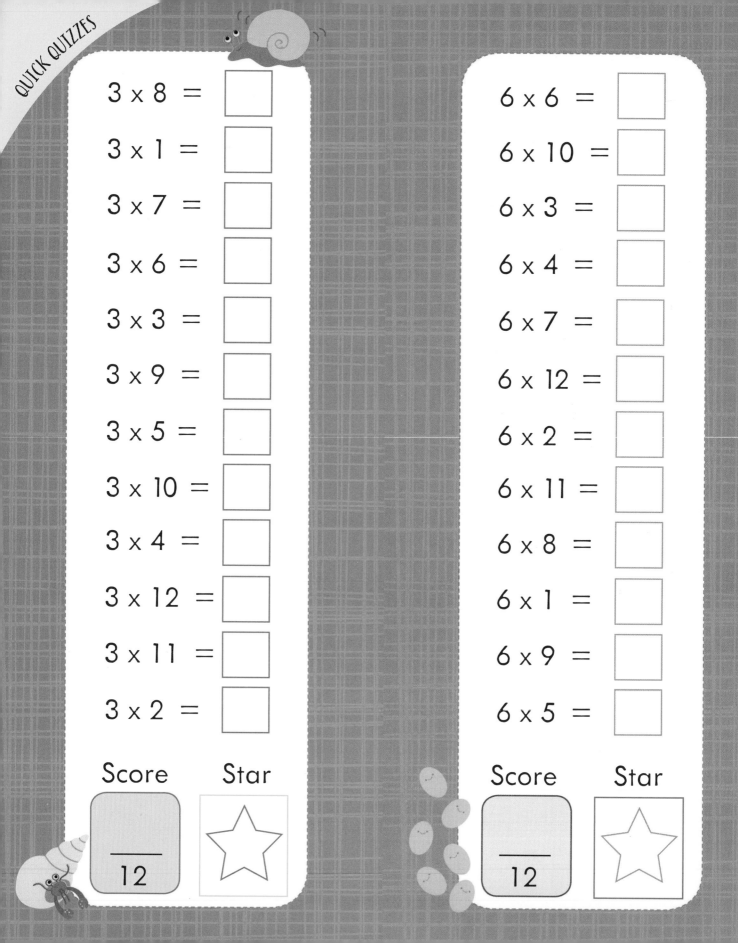

3 x 8 =

3 x 1 =

3 x 7 =

3 x 6 =

3 x 3 =

3 x 9 =

3 x 5 =

3 x 10 =

3 x 4 =

3 x 12 =

3 x 11 =

3 x 2 =

Score   Star

—
12

6 x 6 =

6 x 10 =

6 x 3 =

6 x 4 =

6 x 7 =

6 x 12 =

6 x 2 =

6 x 11 =

6 x 8 =

6 x 1 =

6 x 9 =

6 x 5 =

Score   Star

—
12

7 x 1 =

7 x 9 =

7 x 11 =

7 x 12 =

7 x 6 =

7 x 3 =

7 x 10 =

7 x 7 =

7 x 4 =

7 x 8 =

7 x 5 =

7 x 2 =

Score

$\dfrac{\quad}{12}$

Star

8 x 4 =

8 x 6 =

8 x 9 =

8 x 12 =

8 x 2 =

8 x 7 =

8 x 3 =

8 x 5 =

8 x 8 =

8 x 11 =

8 x 10 =

8 x 1 =

Score

$\dfrac{\quad}{12}$

Star

9x

9 x 1 = 9

9 x 2 = 18

9 x 3 = 27

9 x 4 = 36

9 x 5 = 45

9 x 6 = 54

9 x 7 = 63

9 x 8 = 72

9 x 9 = 81

9 x 10 = 90

9 x 11 = 99

9 x 12 = 108

The digits of each answer add up to 9 (up to 9 x 10).

Fill in the missing numbers.

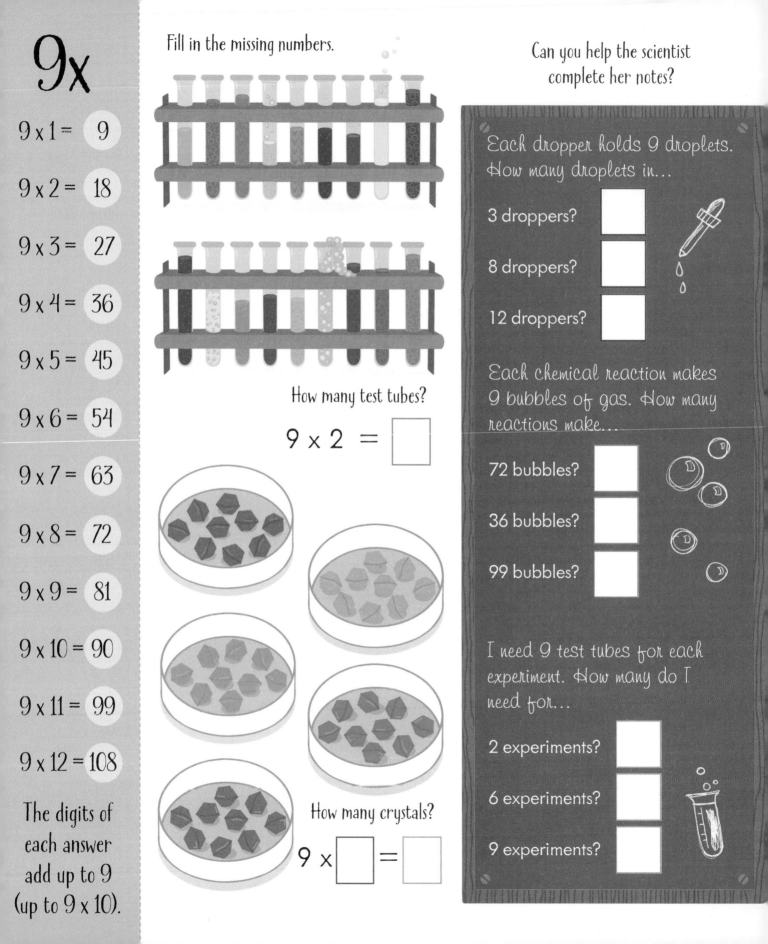

How many test tubes?

9 x 2 = ☐

How many crystals?

9 x ☐ = ☐

Can you help the scientist complete her notes?

Each dropper holds 9 droplets. How many droplets in...

3 droppers? ☐

8 droppers? ☐

12 droppers? ☐

Each chemical reaction makes 9 bubbles of gas. How many reactions make...

72 bubbles? ☐

36 bubbles? ☐

99 bubbles? ☐

I need 9 test tubes for each experiment. How many do I need for...

2 experiments? ☐

6 experiments? ☐

9 experiments? ☐

Pop the bubbles that aren't in the 9 times table by drawing an X over them.

73 18 45 36 62 81 42 99 85 19 27

Fill the flasks to the correct levels.
The first one has been filled already.

9 × 3
9 × 4
9 × 7
9 × 9

Draw explosions on the flasks
which match these answers:

54 72 18
99 90 108

9 × 6   9 × 1   9 × 11   9 × 10   9 × 2   9 × 9   9 × 8   9 × 12

7x 8x 9x

The cake factory packs cupcakes into boxes of 8.
How many cakes has this machine packed already? ....

Each Cake-O-Matic machine runs for 7 hours every day.
Write in the number of cakes each machine will make in a day.

4 cakes every hour

Number of cakes =

6 cakes every hour

Number of cakes =

3 cakes every hour

Number of cakes =

The cake factory is taking orders. How many cakes does each person want?

I need enough
cakes for 7 people
to have 2 each.

....
cakes

Can I have 9 chocolate
cakes, 9 lemon cakes
and 9 vanilla cakes?

....
cakes

Please can I have
4 boxes with
8 cakes in each?

....
cakes

Decorate these cupcakes, following the icing guide below.

Multiples of 7 = blue
Multiples of 8 = purple
Multiples of 9 = yellow

The decorating machine splits the decorations equally between 9 cupcakes. Fill in the boxes...

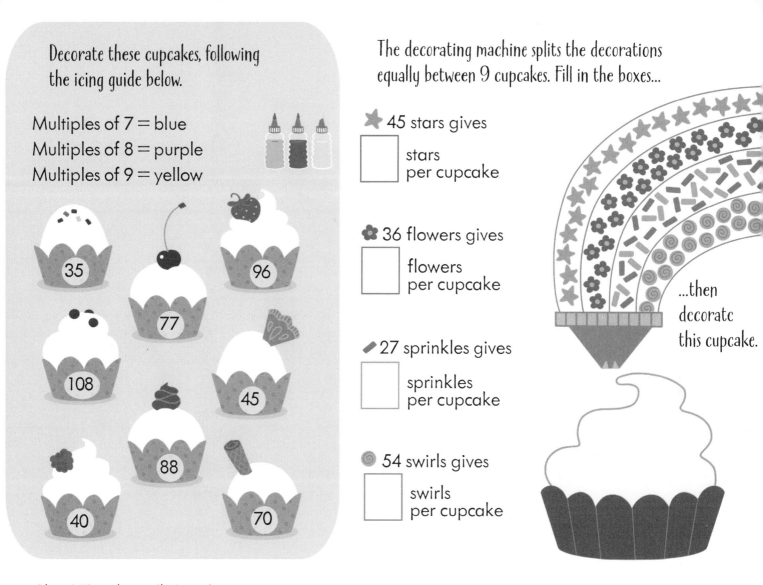

★ 45 stars gives

[ ] stars per cupcake

❁ 36 flowers gives

[ ] flowers per cupcake

✦ 27 sprinkles gives

[ ] sprinkles per cupcake

◉ 54 swirls gives

[ ] swirls per cupcake

...then decorate this cupcake.

Oh no! Flour has spilled on these recipes.
Fill in the missing numbers, following the times tables.

To make 7 cakes:

7 eggs
14 oranges
___ lemons
___ cups of sugar
35 cups of flour

To make 8 cakes:

8 eggs
___ oranges
24 lemons
___ cups of sugar
___ cups of flour

To make 9 cakes:

9 eggs
___ oranges
___ lemons
36 cups of sugar
___ cups of flour

11x

11 x 1 = 11
11 x 2 = 22
11 x 3 = 33
11 x 4 = 44
11 x 5 = 55
11 x 6 = 66
11 x 7 = 77
11 x 8 = 88
11 x 9 = 99
11 x 10 = 110
11 x 11 = 121
11 x 12 = 132

Up to 11 x 9, the two digits in each answer are the same.

Fill in the missing numbers.

How many wheels?

11 x 3 = ☐

How many diamonds?

11 x ☐ = ☐

The car which has an *even* answer will win the race. Can you figure out which one, and circle it?

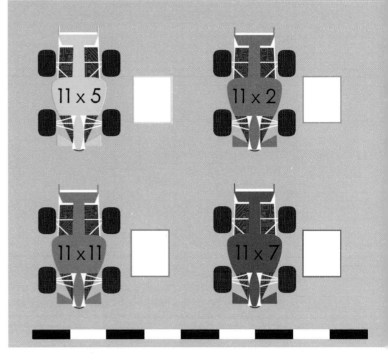

11 x 5 ☐   11 x 2 ☐

11 x 11 ☐   11 x 7 ☐

Can you find a route from the middle of the wheel to the edge, only passing numbers in the 11 times table?

--- Finish here.

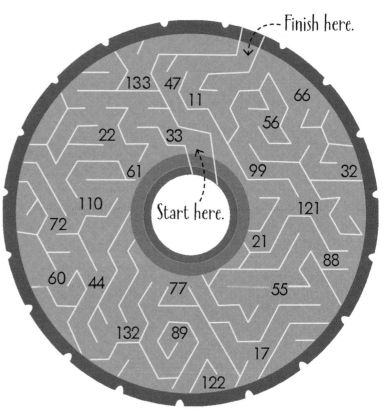

133 47
11
66
56
22 33
99 32
61
110 121
72 Start here.
21
88
60 44
77 55
132 89
17
122

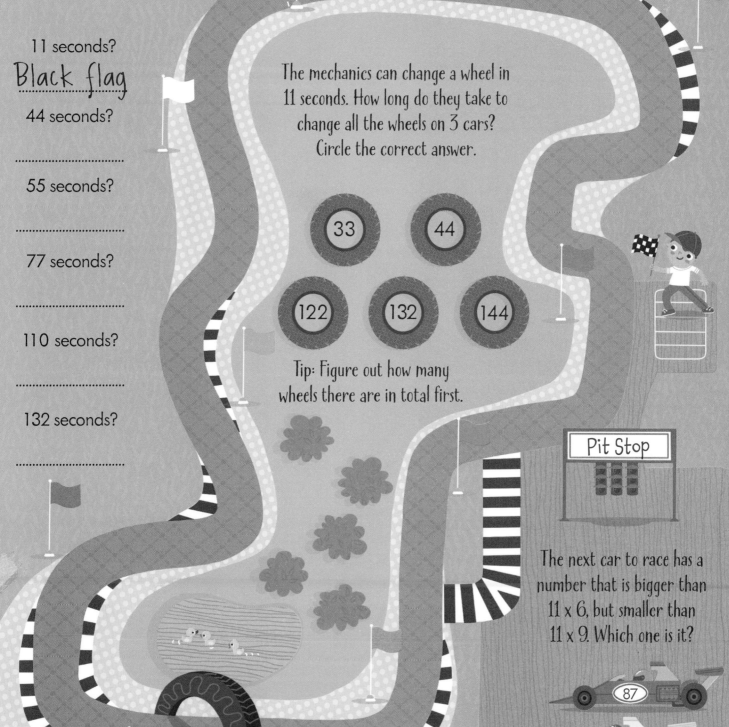

The car speeds between each flag in 11 seconds. Where will it be from the start in...

11 seconds?
Black flag

44 seconds?
....

55 seconds?
....

77 seconds?
....

110 seconds?
....

132 seconds?
....

The mechanics can change a wheel in 11 seconds. How long do they take to change all the wheels on 3 cars? Circle the correct answer.

33   44

122   132   144

Tip: Figure out how many wheels there are in total first.

Pit Stop

The next car to race has a number that is bigger than 11 x 6, but smaller than 11 x 9. Which one is it?

87

100

62

35

12x

12 x 1 = 12

12 x 2 = 24

12 x 3 = 36

12 x 4 = 48

12 x 5 = 60

12 x 6 = 72

12 x 7 = 84

12 x 8 = 96

12 x 9 = 108

12 x 10 = 120

12 x 11 = 132

12 x 12 = 144

Remember, the only one you haven't seen before is 12 x 12.

Fill in the missing numbers.

How many stars?

12 x 3 = ☐

How many windows?

12 x ☐ = ☐

Paint the knights' shields following the guide below.

12 x 4
12 x 3
12 x 9

132   24
144

12 x 1
12 x 8
12 x 10

12
72
108

12 x 7
12 x 5
12 x 12

12 x 6
12 x 11
12 x 2

48
84   96   60

Finish the shopping list for the castle cook. He has 12 hungry knights to feed.

☐ Onions (4 each)

☐ Chickens (2 each)

☐ Potatoes (10 each)

☐ Loaves of bread (3 each)

☐ Apples (6 each)

☐ Sausages (5 each)

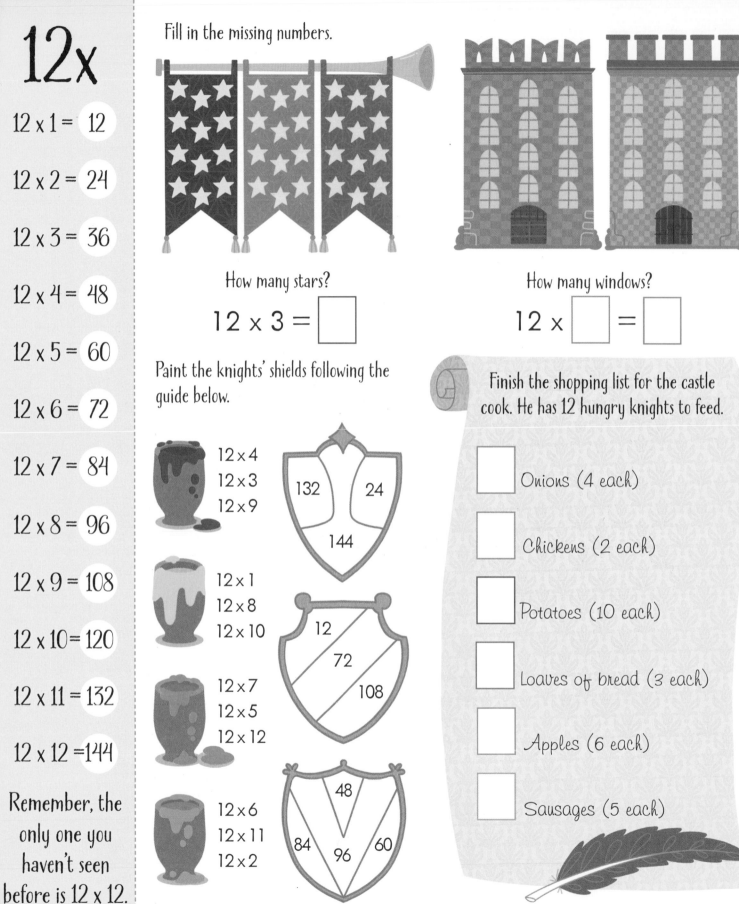

Help the knight escape from the labyrinth.
Only numbers in the 12x table are safe to pass.

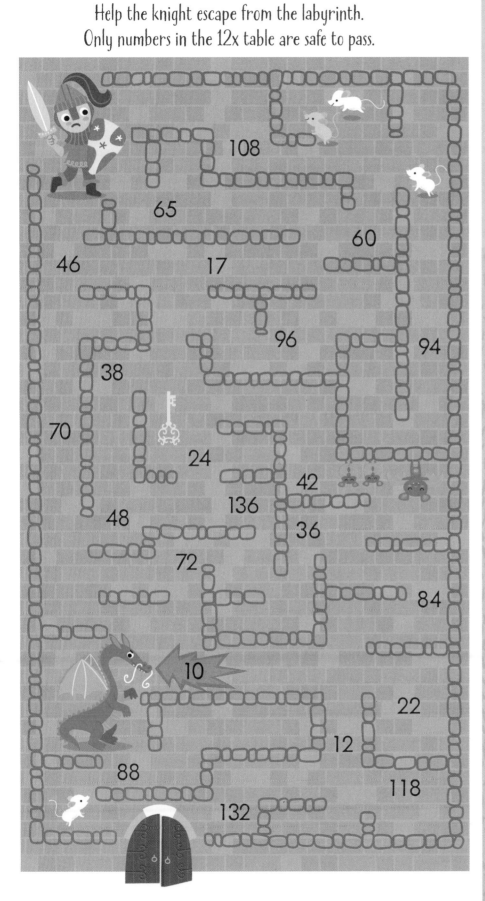

How many points has each archer scored?

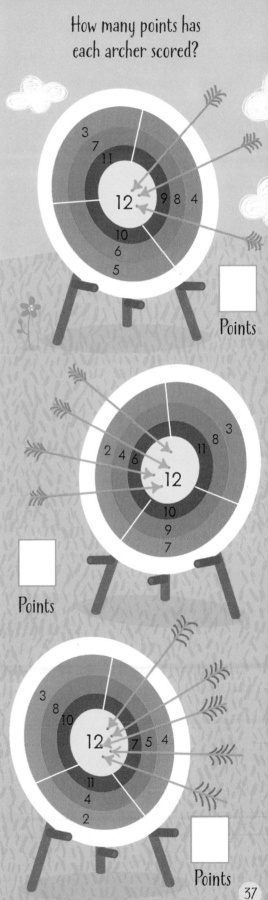

Points

Points

Points

9 x 11 =

9 x 9 =

9 x 4 =

9 x 12 =

9 x 7 =

9 x 1 =

9 x 8 =

9 x 3 =

9 x 6 =

9 x 10 =

9 x 2 =

9 x 5 =

Score

Star

—
12

11 x 2 =

11 x 11 =

11 x 3 =

11 x 10 =

11 x 1 =

11 x 12 =

11 x 5 =

11 x 4 =

11 x 6 =

11 x 7 =

11 x 9 =

11 x 8 =

Score

Star

—
12

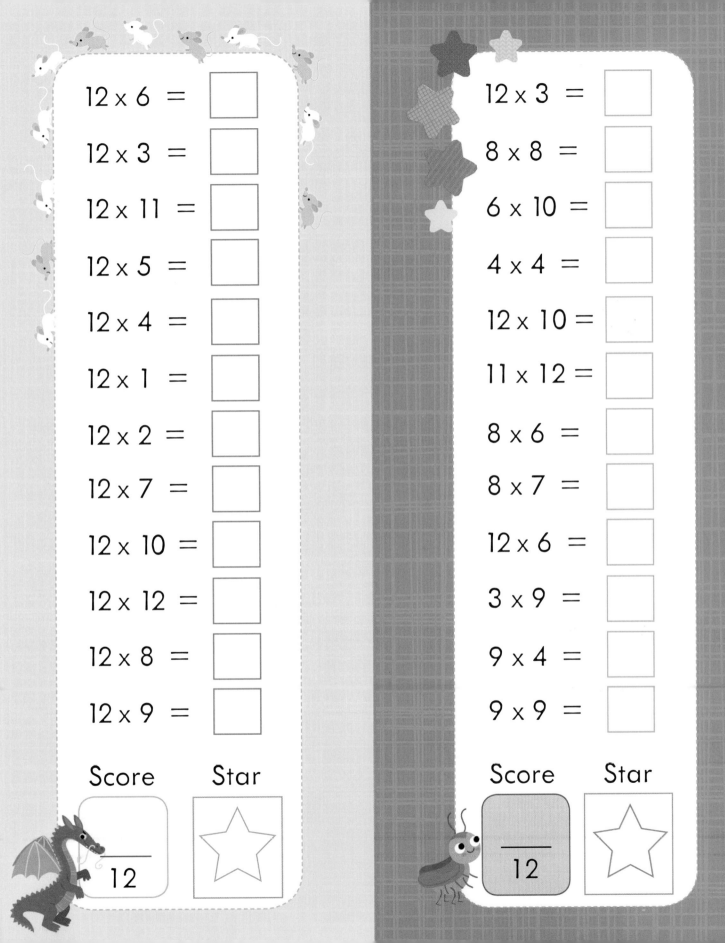

12 x 6 =

12 x 3 =

12 x 11 =

12 x 5 =

12 x 4 =

12 x 1 =

12 x 2 =

12 x 7 =

12 x 10 =

12 x 12 =

12 x 8 =

12 x 9 =

Score

Star

12

12 x 3 =

8 x 8 =

6 x 10 =

4 x 4 =

12 x 10 =

11 x 12 =

8 x 6 =

8 x 7 =

12 x 6 =

3 x 9 =

9 x 4 =

9 x 9 =

Score

Star

12

Treasure island

Solve the clues to steer the pirate ship across the ocean to the island filled with treasure.

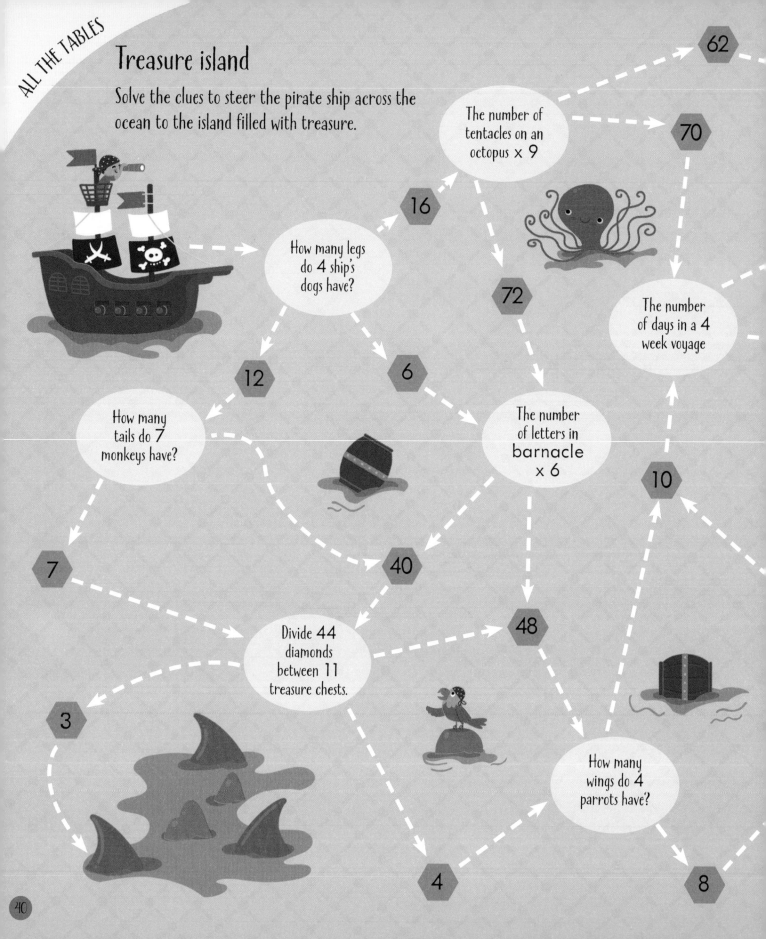

62

70

The number of tentacles on an octopus x 9

16

How many legs do 4 ship's dogs have?

72

The number of days in a 4 week voyage

12

6

How many tails do 7 monkeys have?

The number of letters in **barnacle** x 6

10

40

7

Divide 44 diamonds between 11 treasure chests.

48

3

How many wings do 4 parrots have?

4

8

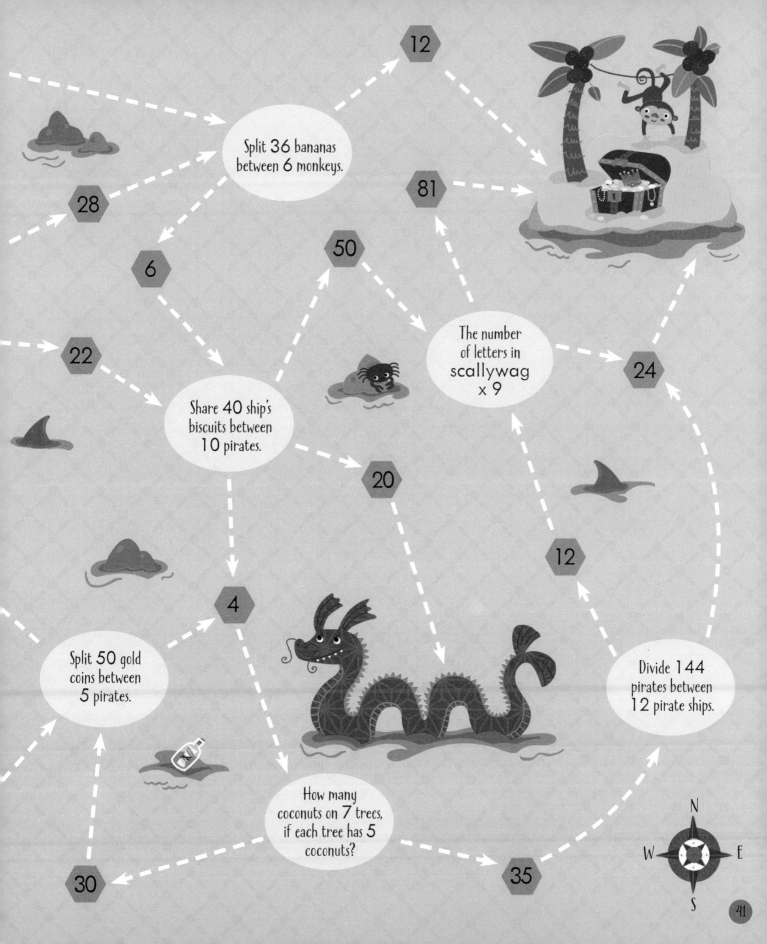

12

Split **36** bananas between **6** monkeys.

81

28

6

50

22

The number of letters in **scallywag** × 9

24

Share **40** ship's biscuits between **10** pirates.

20

12

4

Split **50** gold coins between **5** pirates.

Divide **144** pirates between **12** pirate ships.

How many coconuts on **7** trees, if each tree has **5** coconuts?

30

35

N
W   E
S

41

At the fair

Figure out the score for knocking down each matching pair by multiplying their numbers together.

Can you fill in the missing numbers on the flags?

9 18 27

11 7 8 6

3 1 2 5

⊘ = 22   ⊘ =

⊘ =   ⊘ =

Finish the numbers on the 'Test Your Strength' game.

TEST YOUR STRENGTH

-144
-132
-
-
-96
-
-72
-
-
-36
-24
-12

Fill in the windows and wheels using this key.

Do you notice a pattern?

48 24 60 12
72 18 36 16

6 x 6

3 x 8

12 x 3

4 x 12 2 x 6

4 x 4 5 x 12

3 x 6 8 x 9

63 81

To win me, hit all the coconuts in the 8x table.

4 6 28 33 20

24 8 12 9 16 1

To win me, hit all the coconuts in the 4x table.

How many hits to win the lion? ☐   How many hits to win the panda? ☐

Which duck wins the most points?

🦆 Red duck – multiply the number by 7.
🦆 Yellow duck – multiply the number by 5.

8 4 9
11 2 7 12 3

2 × 12
9 × 4
4 × 6
8 × 2   10 × 6
2 × 9   12 × 6
8 × 6   4 × 3

Creepy-crawlies

Shade in the answers on the honeycomb to help the bee find a route through the hive. Cross out the questions as you find them.

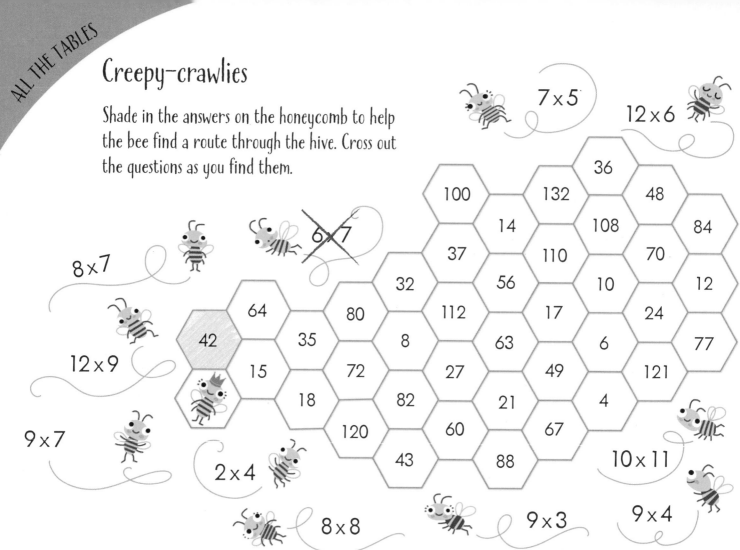

7 × 5

12 × 6

6 × 7

8 × 7

12 × 9

9 × 7

2 × 4

8 × 8

9 × 3

9 × 4

10 × 11

Which pair of bugs wins the race? Multiply their numbers together.
The pair with the biggest number wins — which pair will it be?

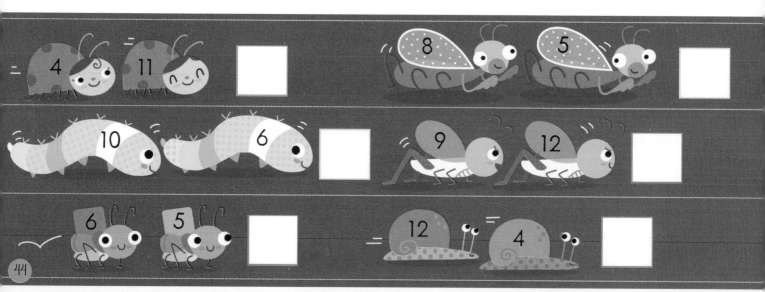

What shape are the fireflies making in the night sky? Find out by linking up the answers to the questions in the crescent moon in order.

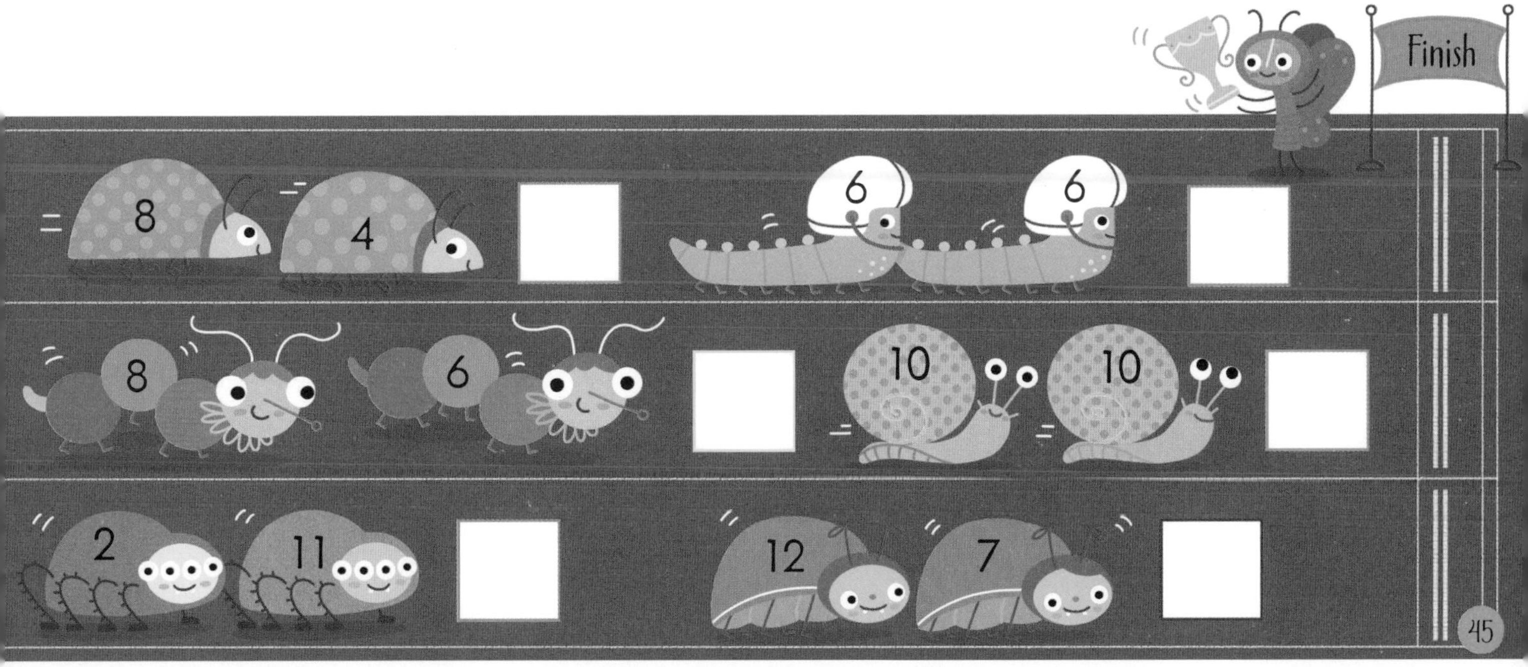

Questions in the crescent moon:
6 × 6
9 × 5
5 × 6
4 × 8
9 × 10
6 × 9
8 × 3
12 × 6
2 × 8
4 × 11
2 × 7
8 × 12
4 × 9

Stars in the sky: 22, 30, 99, 21, 36, 105, 89, 15, 46, 45, 80, 32, 77, 33, 31, 96, 90, 52, 54, 23, 14, 88, 102, 4, 44, 72, 24, 18, 62, 16, 70, 112

Finish

8   4   □

6   6   □

8   6   □   10   10   □

2   11   □   12   7   □

45

Times tables town

Can you draw a route for the van to deliver these letters in the following order?

8 x 5

9 x 7

6 x 6

5 x 11

8 x 4

12 x 9

2 x 10

7 x 6

4 x 4

40

63

49

64

36

72

108

55

18

24

70

32

Circle the correct answers to these puzzles.

Which letter is going to a house with a red front door?

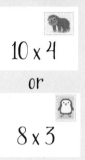

10 x 4

or

8 x 3

Which letter is going to a house with a blue roof?

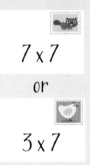

7 x 7

or

3 x 7

Which letter is going to a house with two chimneys?

2 x 3

or

4 x 8

47

Air show

Fill in the times tables on the planes' banners.

7x

21

24

Decorate the hot air balloons so that...

...numbers in the 5x table are red.
...numbers in the 7x table are yellow.
...numbers in the 9x table are purple.
...numbers in the 11x table are green.
...numbers in the 12x table are pink.

11
25
96
27

9   28
22   10

15   14
66   54

56
33
24
40

48
121   49
81

12
18   30
42

| 28 | | | | | | | |

| 120 | 132 | |

Shade in the helicopter propellers, using the clues below.

The helicopter with a number bigger than 9 x 11 has a yellow propeller.

54

20

The one that's smaller than 8 x 3 but bigger than 4 x 4 has a green propeller.

36

The red propeller goes with the number equal to 6 x 6 and 12 x 3.

100

The helicopter with the blue propeller is bigger than 10 x 5 but smaller than 7 x 8.

On safari

Solve the puzzles to guide the trucks on their safari. Where does each truck end up?

Start here

7 blue trucks can carry 42 people. How many people on each truck?

9

Share 45 insects between 5 meerkats.

Start here

Each red truck has 4 wheels. How many wheels do 8 have?

8

20

7

30

32

How many legs do 5 giraffes have?

Share 121 leaves between 11 giraffes.

7

8

56

The number of letters in **crocodile** x 12

8 snakes have 64 spots. altogether. How many spots does 1 snake have?

10

108

20

7

How many ears do 10 elephants have?

Share 25 fish between 5 crocodiles.

5

The number of letters in **rhinoceros** x 7

80

There are 4 lion families, each with 2 cubs. How many cubs are there altogether?

8

12

70

4

36

18

Flamingos like to stand on 1 leg. How many legs do 12 flamingos stand on?

How many paws do 9 tigers have?

80

12

15

11

The number of letters in **baboon** x 9

57

6 people each take 3 photos of the leopards. How many do they take in total?

18

54

16

Share 42 nuts between 6 monkeys.

How many hooves do 4 zebras have?

7

22

20

JUNGLE CAMPSITE

Message in a bottle

Can you decode these two messages? Use the key and write the letters in the circles to find out what they say.

4×3 ◯
4×12 ◯
3×8 ◯
6×10 ◯
2×10 ◯
12×7 ◯
6×4 ◯

4×4 ◯
5×8 ◯
6×2 ◯
12×6 ◯
4×8 ◯
5×12 ◯
4×10 ◯
4×9 ◯

6×12 ◯
5×6 ◯
2×12 ◯
9×12 ◯
2×6 ◯
11×12 ◯

KEY

12 = a
16 = b
20 = c
24 = e
25 = g
30 = h
32 = i
33 = j
35 = k
36 = n
40 = o
48 = r
60 = s
72 = t
84 = u
108 = w
132 = y

6×6 ◯
10×4 ◯
8×9 ◯
3×10 ◯
3×4 ◯
3×12 ◯
7×5 ◯
5×12 ◯

12×2 ◯
12×3 ◯
11×3 ◯
8×5 ◯
12×11 ◯
8×4 ◯
9×4 ◯
5×5 ◯

9×8 ◯
10×3 ◯
8×3 ◯
2×8 ◯
4×6 ◯
4×3 ◯
5×4 ◯
6×5 ◯

Ferry trip

Follow the order of the questions on the right, to draw on the route for the ferry to get back to shore, visiting all the islands on the way.

3 x 5
3 x 10
8 x 8
5 x 5
5 x 11
2 x 7
6 x 8
3 x 4
4 x 7
5 x 12
7 x 10
3 x 9
9 x 4
2 x 4
9 x 12
8 x 10
4 x 11
4 x 5
4 x 8
2 x 11
3 x 6
5 x 8

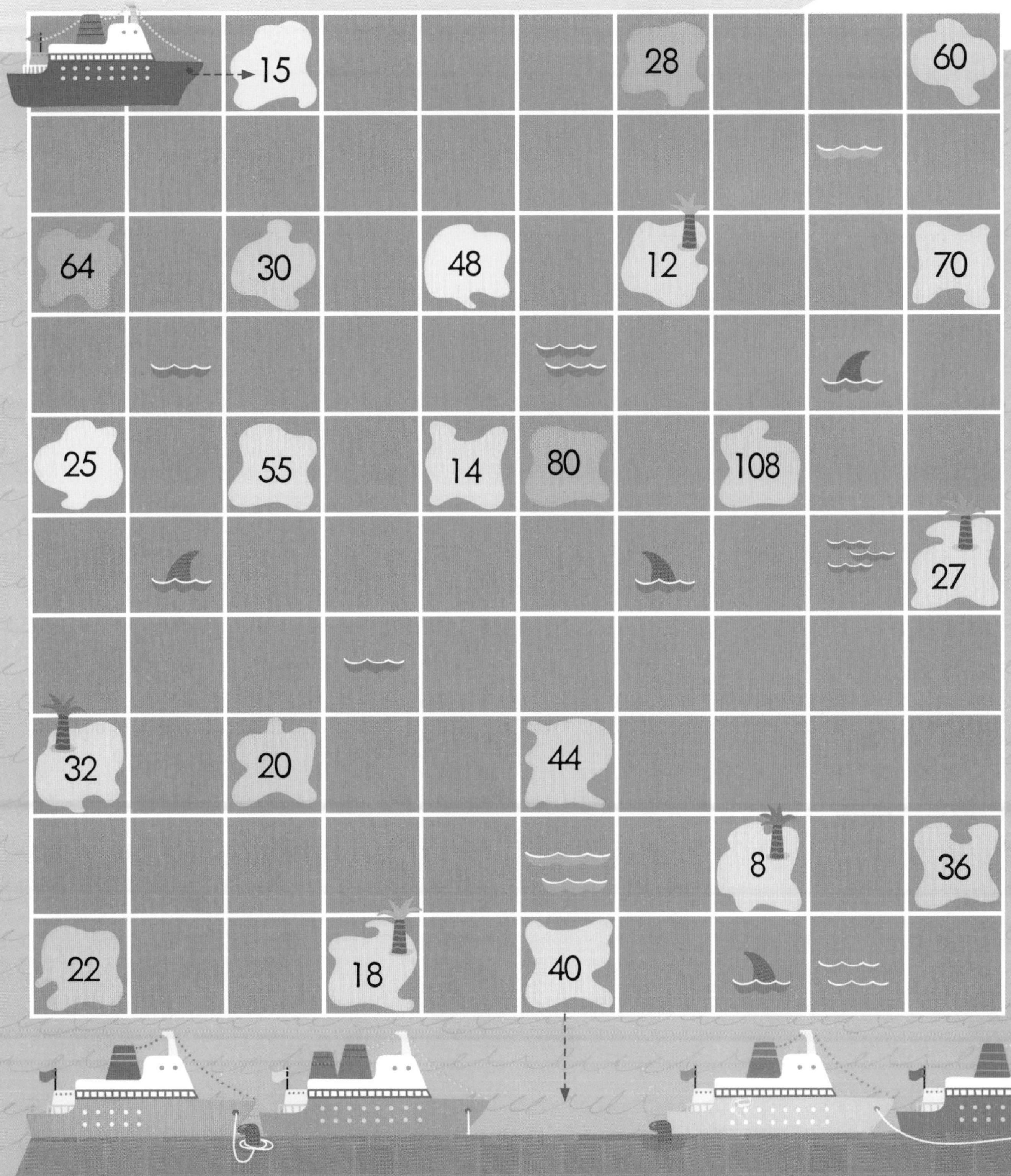

15
28
60
64
30
48
12
70
25
55
14
80
108
27
32
20
44
8
36
22
18
40

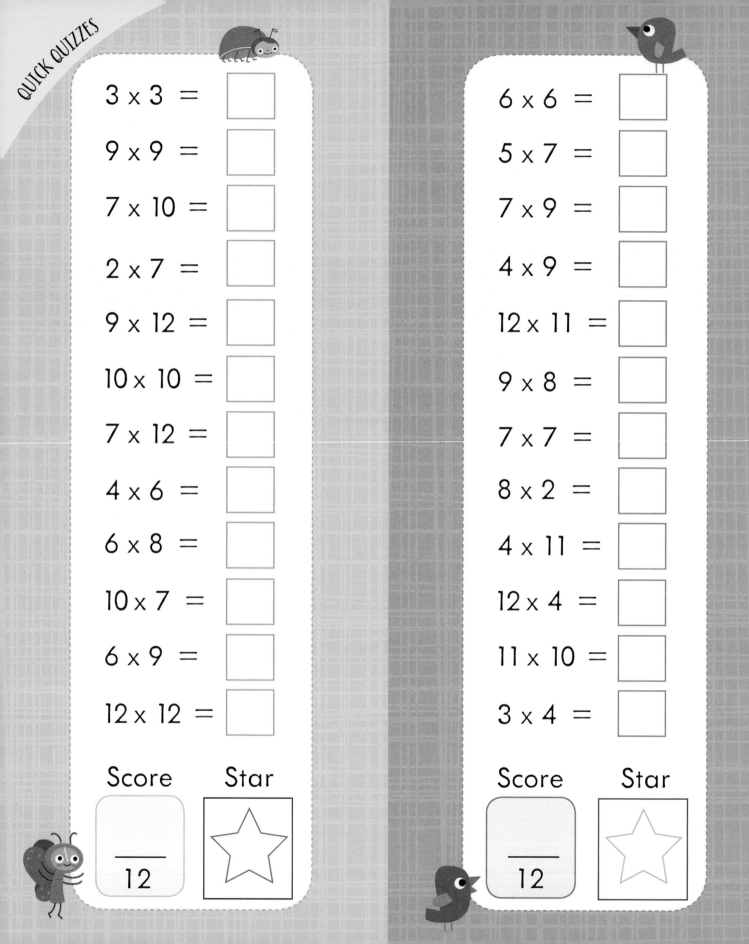

3 x 3 =

9 x 9 =

7 x 10 =

2 x 7 =

9 x 12 =

10 x 10 =

7 x 12 =

4 x 6 =

6 x 8 =

10 x 7 =

6 x 9 =

12 x 12 =

Score

___
12

Star

6 x 6 =

5 x 7 =

7 x 9 =

4 x 9 =

12 x 11 =

9 x 8 =

7 x 7 =

8 x 2 =

4 x 11 =

12 x 4 =

11 x 10 =

3 x 4 =

Score

___
12

Star

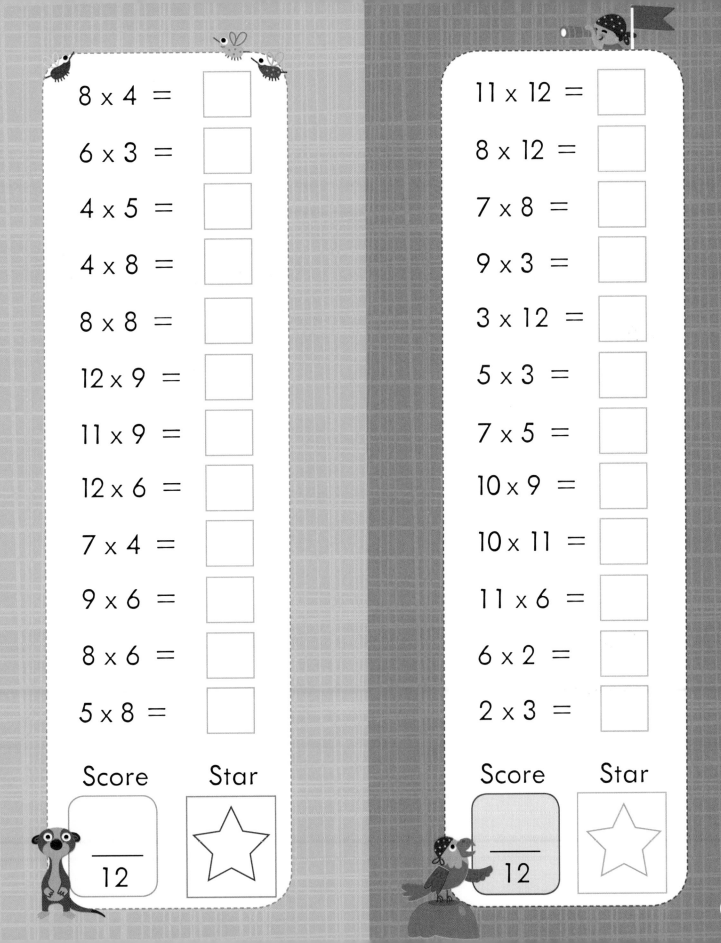

8 x 4 =

6 x 3 =

4 x 5 =

4 x 8 =

8 x 8 =

12 x 9 =

11 x 9 =

12 x 6 =

7 x 4 =

9 x 6 =

8 x 6 =

5 x 8 =

Score

Star

$\dfrac{}{12}$

11 x 12 =

8 x 12 =

7 x 8 =

9 x 3 =

3 x 12 =

5 x 3 =

7 x 5 =

10 x 9 =

10 x 11 =

11 x 6 =

6 x 2 =

2 x 3 =

Score

Star

$\dfrac{}{12}$

Number puzzles

Fill in the missing numbers, so the touching corners have matching questions and answers.

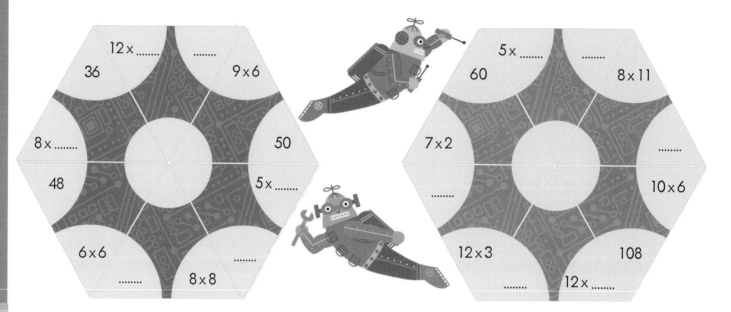

The numbers in the circles on these switchboards are multiplied together to make the number in the square between them. Can you fill in the gaps?

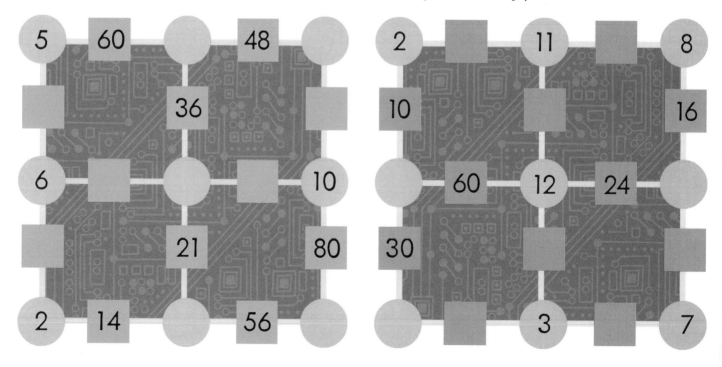

Find the biggest multiple of 12.

84   60
90   45
36   125

Find the biggest multiple of 7.

77   89
54   56
14   50

Find the biggest multiple of 5.

32   35
55   48
72   15

Shade in the two circles that you'd multiply together
to make the number in the middle of the robots.

3
24
8   4

2
14
7   8

7
35
9   5

11
110
10   9

6
30
5   10

6
64
8   8

Fill in the outer rings by multiplying each
number by the times table in the middle.

21

3   5
12   6
11   7x
10   8
9

12   2   4
10   5
9x
9   6
7

Answers
4-5 2x table

2x4 = 8 worms
2x6 = 12 acorns
2x3 = 6 wings

8 butterflies make 4 pairs. 16 butterflies make 8 pairs. 10 butterflies make 5 pairs.

The frog eats the flies with the numbers: 4, 18, 14, 22, 10, 6

The spider can spin 16 webs.

The pink caterpillar's numbers are:
  18, **16**, 14, 12, **10**
The yellow caterpillar's numbers are:
  12, **14**, 16, **18**, 20, **22**
The purple caterpillar's numbers are:
  4, **6**, 8, 10, **12**

6-7 4x table

4x3 = 12 legs
4x2 = 8 bones
4x4 = 16 spots

The iguanas' medals from left to right say: 36, 28, 48, 44

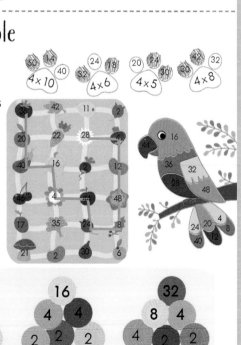

8-9 More practice (2x, 4x)

The player's number is 10.
The sunshine shirt with 24 on it is left.

20 sports socks = 10 pairs
10 gloves = 5 pairs
8 mittens = 4 pairs
16 hiking socks = 8 pairs

12 weeks = 6 boxes and 3 bottles
16 weeks = 8 boxes and 4 bottles
24 weeks = 12 boxes and 6 bottles

The sock with stripes that's hanging on peg number 8 is in the wrong place.

10-11 5x table

5x3 = 15 lights   5x4 = 20 dials   5x2 = 10 wheels

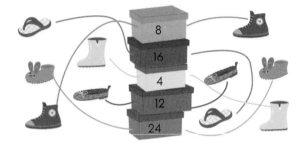

The trail leads to this robot.

12-13 10x table

10x5 = 50 spikes 10x6 = 60 teeth 10x3 = 30 eyes

There are 70 mini-monsters in 7 puddles,
90 mini-monsters in 9 puddles and
120 mini-monsters in 12 puddles.

11 squirts scare 110 monsters, 5 squirts scare
50 monsters, 2 squirts scare 20 monsters.

A big monster can gobble 30 mini-monsters in 3
minutes, 60 in 6 minutes and 100 in 10 minutes.

These monsters are splatted:

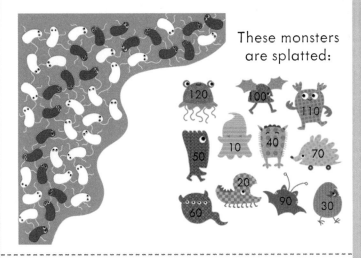

14-15 More practice (5x, 10x)

The alien with the number 35 is chosen for the space mission.

The crater puzzles are:
5x3 = 15   10x6 = 60
10x9 = 90   5x7 = 35

The answers on the planets from left to right are:
5x4 = 20 days
5x2 = 10 days
5 planets
30 days
45 days

16-17 Quick Quizzes

2x2 = 4	4x10 = 40	5x5 = 25	10x8 = 80
2x4 = 8	4x7 = 28	5x9 = 45	10x9 = 90
2x6 = 12	4x5 = 20	5x11 = 55	10x3 = 30
2x11 = 22	4x2 = 8	5x2 = 10	10x6 = 60
2x3 = 6	4x6 = 24	5x6 = 30	10x4 = 40
2x1 = 2	4x12 = 48	5x3 = 15	10x12 = 120
2x10 = 20	4x9 = 36	5x10 = 50	10x10 = 100
2x12 = 24	4x11 = 44	5x8 = 40	10x2 = 20
2x9 = 18	4x3 = 12	5x4 = 20	10x5 = 50
2x5 = 10	4x1 = 4	5x12 = 60	10x11 = 110
2x8 = 16	4x4 = 16	5x7 = 35	10x1 = 10
2x7 = 14	4x8 = 32	5x1 = 5	10x7 = 70

18-19 3x table

3x2 = 6 flags
3x3 = 9 flowers
3x4 = 12 scoops

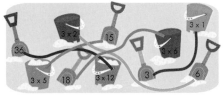

These shells aren't in the 3 times table: 14, 23, 32

The number pattern is the 3 times table:
3, **6**, **9**, 12, **15**, **18**, 21, 24, **27**, **30**, **33**, 36

20-21 6x table

6x3 = 18 cartons
6x8 = 48 muffins
6x6 = 36 bagels

Count the eggs using the 6 times table: 6, 12, 18, 24, 30, 36, 42, 48, 54, 60, 66, 72

Shopping list:
12 sandwiches
36 tomatoes
24 breadsticks
18 cereal bars
60 cherries
6 apples

There are 3 coconut cookies, 2 chocolate cookies and 4 cherry cookies.

These groceries are in the 6 times table:

22-23 More practice (3x, 6x)

These shuttlecocks are in the
3x and 6x tables:
12, 6, 24, 18, 36, 30

The basketball with the number
18 is left.

The skier with the blue flags
gets 42 points.
The skier with the red flags
gets 24 points.

54
6 9
2 3 3

36
6 6
3 2 3

18
6 3
2 3 1

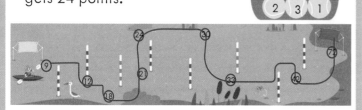

24-25 7x table

7x2 = 14 bells
7x3 = 21 fish

Checkpoint 3: 21 days
Checkpoint 5: 35 days
Checkpoint 7: 49 days
63 days = Checkpoint 9
77 days = Checkpoint 11

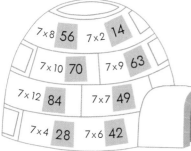

7x8 56   7x2 14
7x10 70   7x9 63
7x12 84   7x7 49
7x4 28   7x6 42

She catches
these fish: 56,
21, 42, 63,
35, 84, 70

Connect the
dots: a seal
is swimming
under the ice.

26-27 8x table

8x3 = 24 tentacles
8x6 = 48 spikes

The seahorse with 8x2 has the smallest number.
The clownfish with 96 has the biggest number.

28-29 Quick Quizzes

3x8 = 24	6x6 = 36	7x1 = 7	8x4 = 32
3x1 = 3	6x10 = 60	7x9 = 63	8x6 = 48
3x7 = 21	6x3 = 18	7x11 = 77	8x9 = 72
3x6 = 18	6x4 = 24	7x12 = 84	8x12 = 96
3x3 = 9	6x7 = 42	7x6 = 42	8x2 = 16
3x9 = 27	6x12 = 72	7x3 = 21	8x7 = 56
3x5 = 15	6x2 = 12	7x10 = 70	8x3 = 24
3x10 = 30	6x11 = 66	7x7 = 49	8x5 = 40
3x4 = 12	6x8 = 48	7x4 = 28	8x8 = 64
3x12 = 36	6x1 = 6	7x8 = 56	8x11 = 88
3x11 = 33	6x9 = 54	7x5 = 35	8x10 = 80
3x2 = 6	6x5 = 30	7x2 = 14	8x1 = 8

30-31 9x table

9x2 = 18 test tubes
9x5 = 45 crystals

3 droppers hold 27 droplets. 8 droppers hold
72 droplets. 12 droppers hold 108 droplets.

8 reactions make 72 bubbles. 4 reactions make
36 bubbles. 11 reactions make 99 bubbles.

She needs 18 test tubes for 2 experiments,
54 test tubes for 6 experiments and 81 test
tubes for 9 experiments.

The bubbles not in the 9x table are:
73, 62, 42, 85, 19

32-33 More practice (7x, 8x, 9x)

There are 8 cake boxes, so the machine has packed 64 cakes.

From left to right, the red machines make 28 cakes, 42 cakes, 21 cakes.

From left to right, the people want 14 cakes, 27 cakes and 32 cakes.

The cupcake should have 5 stars, 4 flowers, 3 sprinkles and 6 swirls.

35 96 77 108 45 88 40 70

To make 7 cakes:
7 eggs
14 oranges
21 lemons
28 cups of sugar
35 cups of flour

To make 8 cakes:
8 eggs
16 oranges
24 lemons
32 cups of sugar
40 cups of flour

To make 9 cakes:
9 eggs
18 oranges
27 lemons
36 cups of sugar
45 cups of flour

34-35 11x table

11x3 = 33 wheels
11x8 = 88 diamonds

The car will be at these flags:
11 seconds = black
44 seconds = orange
55 seconds = yellow
77 seconds = blue
110 seconds = black
132 seconds = pink

11x5   11x2   11x11   11x7

It takes the mechanics 132 seconds to change all the wheels.

This is the next car.

87

36-37 12x table

12x3 = 36 stars
12x2 = 24 windows

Shopping list:
48 onions
24 chickens
120 potatoes
36 loaves of bread
72 apples
60 sausages

132 24 144

12 72 108

48 84 96 60

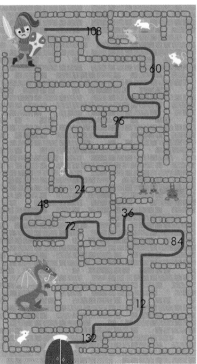

From top to bottom, the archers win 36, 48, 60.

38-39 Quick Quizzes

9x11 = 99	11x2 = 22	12x6 = 72	12x3 = 36
9x9 = 81	11x11 = 121	12x3 = 36	8x8 = 64
9x4 = 36	11x3 = 33	12x11 = 132	6x10 = 60
9x12 = 108	11x10 = 110	12x5 = 60	4x4 = 16
9x7 = 63	11x1 = 11	12x4 = 48	12x10 = 120
9x1 = 9	11x12 = 132	12x1 = 12	11x12 = 132
9x8 = 72	11x5 = 55	12x2 = 24	8x6 = 48
9x3 = 27	11x4 = 44	12x7 = 84	8x7 = 56
9x6 = 54	11x6 = 66	12x10 = 120	12x6 = 72
9x10 = 90	11x7 = 77	12x12 = 144	3x9 = 27
9x2 = 18	11x9 = 99	12x8 = 96	9x4 = 36
9x5 = 45	11x8 = 88	12x9 = 108	9x9 = 81

40-41 Treasure island

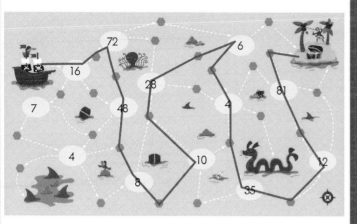

42-43 At the fair

The 9 times table is on the flags: 9, **18**, 27, **36**, **45**, **54**, 63, **72**, 81, **90**, **99**, **108**

The 12 times table is on the 'Test Your Strength' Game: 12, **24**, 36, **48**, 60, 72, **84**, 96, **108**, 120, 132, 144

You need 3 hits to win the lion and 7 hits to win the panda.

This duck wins the most points.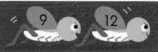

This is the pattern on the train.

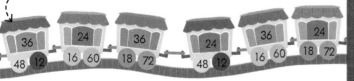

44-45 Creepy-crawlies

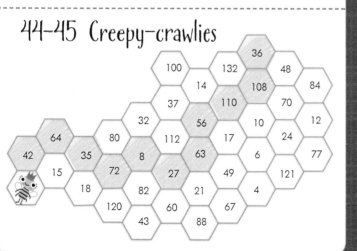

This pair of bugs wins the race.

46-47 Times tables town

8 x 3 — This letter goes to the house with the red front door.

3 x 7 — This letter goes to the house with the yellow front door.

2 x 3 — This letter goes to the house with two chimneys.

48-49 Air show

The 7x banner: 7, **14**, 21, **28**, **35**, **42**, 49, **56**, 63, 70, 77, **84**

The 12x banner: **12**, 24, **36**, **48**, 60, **72**, 84, **96**, **108**, 120, 132, **144**

Helicopter 54 has a blue propeller.
Helicopter 20 has a green propeller.
Helicopter 36 has a red propeller.
Helicopter 100 has a yellow propeller.

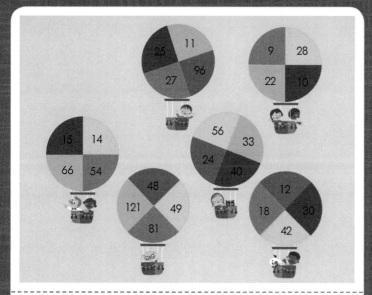

50-51 On safari

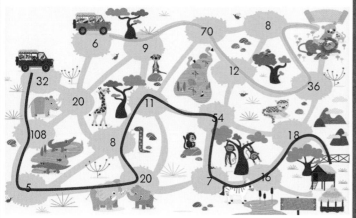

The blue truck ends up at the Lion Look-out.
The red truck ends up at the Jungle Campsite.

52-53 Message in a bottle/Ferry trip

The first message says:
A RESCUE BOAT IS ON THE WAY

The second message says:
NO THANKS ENJOYING THE BEACH

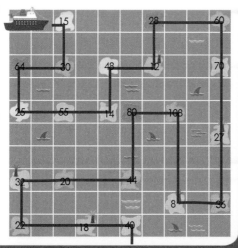

54-55 Quick Quizzes

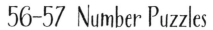

3x3 = 9	6x6 = 36	8x4 = 32	11x12 = 132
9x9 = 81	5x7 = 35	6x3 = 18	8x12 = 96
7x10 = 70	7x9 = 63	4x5 = 20	7x8 = 56
2x7 = 14	4x9 = 36	4x8 = 32	9x3 = 27
9x12 = 108	12x11 = 132	8x8 = 64	3x12 = 36
10x10 = 100	9x8 = 72	12x9 = 108	5x3 = 15
7x12 = 84	7x7 = 49	11x9 = 99	7x5 = 35
4x6 = 24	8x2 = 16	12x6 = 72	10x9 = 90
6x8 = 48	4x11 = 44	7x4 = 28	10x11 = 110
10x7 = 70	12x4 = 48	9x6 = 54	11x6 = 66
6x9 = 54	11x10 = 110	8x6 = 48	6x2 = 12
12x12 = 144	3x4 = 12	5x8 = 40	2x3 = 6

56-57 Number Puzzles

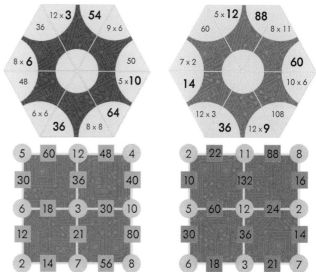

The biggest multiple of 12 is 84. The biggest multiple of 7 is 77. The biggest multiple of 5 is 55.

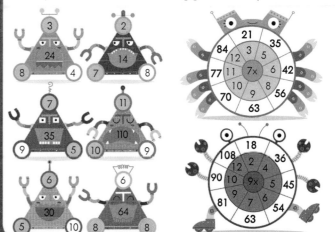

Times Table Square

This times table square can help you find the answers to any times table question. For example, if you want the answer to 7 x 5, run your finger down from the 7 in the red row and along from the 5 in the green column. Where they meet is the answer: 35. Try it out for yourself...

Pick a number in the green column...

...and a number in the red row.

Finding the answer is easy!

The answers repeat either side of this pink line.

X	1	2	3	4	5	6	7	8	9	10	11	12
1	1	2	3	4	5	6	7	8	9	10	11	12
2	2	4	6	8	10	12	14	16	18	20	22	24
3	3	6	9	12	15	18	21	24	27	30	33	36
4	4	8	12	16	20	24	28	32	36	40	44	48
5	5	10	15	20	25	30	35	40	45	50	55	60
6	6	12	18	24	30	36	42	48	54	60	66	72
7	7	14	21	28	35	42	49	56	63	70	77	84
8	8	16	24	32	40	48	56	64	72	80	88	96
9	9	18	27	36	45	54	63	72	81	90	99	108
10	10	20	30	40	50	60	70	80	90	100	110	120
11	11	22	33	44	55	66	77	88	99	110	121	132
12	12	24	36	48	60	72	84	96	108	120	132	144

Edited by Rosie Dickins   Managing Designer: Zoe Wray

First published in 2016 by Usborne Publishing Ltd., Usborne House, 83-85 Saffron Hill, London, EC1N 8RT, England, usborne.com Copyright © 2020, 2016 Usborne Publishing Ltd.